Glean

APR 1 6 2008

NIGHTBOAT BOOKS   COLD SPRING, NEW YORK   2007

Winner of the 2005 Nightboat Poetry Prize

Glean

POEMS BY JOSHUA KRYAH

Library of Congress
Cataloging-in-Publication Data
Kryah, Joshua. 1974 –
Glean : poems / by Joshua Kryah
   p. cm.
ISBN 0-9767185-4-5
I. Title.
PS3611.R885G54 2007
811'.6 — DC22
2006103187

Original printing 2007
Design and typesetting by Amber Withycombe
Text face: Perpetua
Display faces: Formata and The Mix

for Eavan, for Amber

CONTENTS

At the very end of his writing life, D.H. Lawrence addressed himself urgently and with passionate precision to St. John of Patmos and to all the epical disruptions of his Revelation. Now, Joshua Kryah is the first in his own generation to take up the vivid purposes of Lawrence's final passion and precision. His uptake takes the form of a question becoming many questions. In the process, many new tones resound. After we've reaped the whirlwind, what remains to glean? This debut approaches the conundrum and its quiet apocalypse not desperately but, against all precedents (including Lawrence's), lovingly. And such approach is amply rewarded. In the hollow places of our day and depraved natures, Kryah finds not emptiness, but an echoing sound of wings or what he calls in one poem "the drone of our folded hearts." In the waste spaces, he finds a spark just now coming alight—alight for warmth, not for burning; scintillant, not scorching. Crazy as it may sound, in *Glean* we have the love poetry of a terrible aftermath we need not fear after all. *Ce ne peut être que le fin du monde, en avançant.* The use of poetry is the tenderness of courage, inexhaustibly original. I am beholden to Kryah for avowing and evincing just so.

—Donald Revell

God cannot
discontinue—
~~annull~~ himself—
This appalling
trust is at times
all that
remains——
——E.D.

CALLED BACK, CALLED BACK

Acquit me, make me
purblind, unbloomed, a thing that,

when roused,
                    remains dormant, unused, none
among many. As the bulb that persists within its sullen,

despondent mood, alive, but no more, no better
than some kind of senseless meat.

I turn away but wherever I turn I encounter
the same soft refrain —

                    I did not call you, lie back down.
          I did not call, lie back, lie down.

There is death and then
                    there is sleep, or I no longer know who's calling or
what I've heard or what I'll say. As, when roused once more

by your voice-light, its endless drag and weight,
I move

          as a tuber on the verge of swelling, the called-forth,
fruited body, caught between monad and many,

between almost and already.

APPROACH, OPEN

1

What kind of name
                is a name asking, when the one
spoken to, continually attenuated,

does not speak?

Steady affliction,
                my entire person, this embodiment,
what went missing in the first place —

self, samara, the winged fruit.

Called also, *key*.

2

What follows self?

This slow foment of shape, this semblance,
similitude.

This sham,
            a ghost town assembled, so spectral, so fabulous
it will not fade —

                    it's me, it's me, it's me —
The lock fixed in which a voice utters "turn."

3

What was intended?

A form
        in which a name could elicit such trembling,
each limb buffeted and broke and separating.

The self now sundered, now apart.

O help me through the fact of you, unfasten
whatever arrives.

Someone wants in.

AUBADE

Metal is the most honest.

You knock and nothing answers.

A raised fist, an echo,
                    snow sliding sideways
from a tin roof, and the sun gone for days.

The difference between waking and sleeping
has now become no different,
                              the sheets empty
and in knots at the edge of the bed.

By laid bare,
            do you mean you won't bring this up again?
By asking me to come, do you mean to have it out?

I remember a stick leaning in a hallway, a hat
on a table, a narrow road
                        outside a window. The stars
like something I wish I had said earlier.

Now you want that.

What they said.

MY EASTER

Breathbloom, the resurrection lily
spent on its stem,

                    the pale throat thrown back
        announcing—what?

Behold, all at once,
                the flesh-like knot
undone, each petal released, their beauty un-
mistakable and

already gone.

                ~

I will strike the shepherd, and the sheep will be scattered.

                ~

How then explain the resilience of any sacrifice,
when your body becomes

                    a willed disclosure of flight, a transience
arrayed, briefly, to make plain what will soon be lost?

How await the expectant,
                    render such an arrival

when the flower comes apart with an ease and abandon
hands cannot stop,

or don't want to?

~

The lamb that taketh away, taketh away.

~

But what has been taken —
                              your body, broken now,
over and over — has been taken without enmity, without
struggle even.

Only, that grief, this elegy, is remarkable
for its insistence.

                    Appearing to withdraw without yet leaving,
you remain, incur trespass, until such a breach leaves you

errant, wandering in this garden
among your relics, your ruin.

~

I followed, wearing nothing but a linen cloth. They caught hold
of me, but I left the linen and ran off naked.

~

Give me this —
one more day, one more day.

That I might have it,
your just once embrace.

BODY AS GO-BETWEEN

1

Gone.

My body, all the guests.

How will you recognize
                    my nothing, its barest twig,
the charcoal passed from pedestrian to pedestrian?

Transposed, the dark line, my name (somewhere) calling?

2

I agree with charcoal, its scintillant nub.

We became this cipher,

                         code appearing, reappearing, and then
what was sent as invitation to call the body back.

(Who was sent?)

Called to, beseeched, and then

                              awaiting the inviolate guest.
Hands that prayed for hours each day without answering,

they wept.

3

Overmuch, the deluge, its redundancy.

Rain continuing
                to batter the field beyond *field*.
It gave up holes, this body, its porous nature, the lack of it.

The way it held still (though porous).

And escaping all the while (again) the body,
its redundancy.

4

Too small to read from here, each letter, my name.

The white corrupting the white of each syllable—
why the charcoal was passed.

They made signs that resembled digging,
but I was too far above them.

When they got on their knees
to see better, I didn't look back.

HOW WILL YOU RENDER IT, HOW WILL YOU HOLD IT, HOW WILL YOU BURY OR CARRY IT AWAY

Errant

In the empty   rehearsed space   this chapel our hands

folded like so   little else   but us o us praying   and more

gathered to press a name to   the specter   halo of moisture

the one ghost   surely the only ghost

to have graced this town with its wet signature

today the assembled   left to right

the assembled   huddled close and shivering

if ever there was   mention of   before now   comes this

in so familiar a way

we went further and further   coming out

the assembled   the applause   the other side.

Straight (not straight, and broken lines)

This would follow after   but no one told me

move slowly when moving at all

the road a chalk-line   night a faded blue

reach around and touch me   while everything else goes by

because everything you've said I've already forgotten

say something else   then repeat   come close   come closer

the distance between us   now shut in both directions

now only a finger pointing away

before this   my entire life

a stick   leaning against a house.

Church of the Corpus Azul

Threadbare   the lampblack body drawn with carbon

the soul made of horsehair

this pilgrimage leads to a single shade of absence

atonement piebald

penance   ash-faced   leaden

and on the mountain the air

is continually bruised

by prayer

the words   themselves   beating.

Errant

Comes a crow on the back of a horse   gleaning

such hunger from the landscape

makes an image   itself   hungry

meaning this crow   as none other than myself

trying to get to you   before nightfall

before remembering   m'Lord   how contingent upon my wandering

your voice   vanishes ascends descends vanishes again

no rigging beyond its partition

this journey   always so sudden   exits.

Green Hymn

To eulogize   elegy   to mean

erudition continuing throughout everything it touches

until   necessarily   reaching   it

stubborn perch   the crow recedes upon

air   draft   the slow alluvial churn of wings

in tandem   hands fold   into one another

each other   caught   unaware

in prayer   homage

holding fast   though unfinished   perhaps

it can be read   as it is.

THE WOUND IN WHICH THE WORD

Word or words, their folding in.

The field, the fold, I herd them
                              toward, upon, against,
in reply to, face to face with, touching—

                                        you.

The puncture, spot that flecks your skin, slit where the words go,
where they live.

            The sheepfold, their wool shirts marred by red,
one sepulchered body after another, their din.

The clamor of their tongues, their evensong.

I was told to take them in, *reach hither thy hand, and thrust it into my side.*
Only the words then,

            so easily led through it all, *reach hither thy hand*, every one
accounted for, when I reach—perforated, open, the running wound—

                                        you.

HYMENEAL

Blue-lipped, I hear you
singing,

       distant and demure, gathering and then
withdrawn, you repeat, you swear—

              I'll smell thee on the tree.

O HIEROGLYPH *(forgotten word, spread your red lips around me)*

As if the wet vowel might speak.

As if, plundered,
                    it might give up its blank stare, and
suddenly, shudder in my mouth.

We exchange a language
                    dumb as flesh, pressed into and bruised
beyond recognition, its only response the black eye's dull circle of speech.

Blue, blue-brown,
                    each color offset by the surrounding skin,
the calcite thought of your returning again.

I cannot muster
                    what I should have lost, and in the wish gained
more steadfast: your curio, what swings from a locket upon my chest,

a message that now only speaks
with its fist.

THE WHITE NO WHERE

There is this deciduousness inside me.

Shedding or losing
                the scion, my heart, remains adamant, repeating
against what does not wish to keep it.

The body (my body)
                erases, from repetition, what was once
the reason, now the result of such fury —

                                having been led so far to encounter
this never-ending whiteness, each artery, blended, beats against it,

as if to create,
                out of motion, out of the sickness of motion,
a color to contrast what consumes it:

o opaque world, de-veined limb, you my Lord.

CHURCH OF THE WHITE CORPOREAL

I tore it off, soaked it
in my mouth.

>   It assuaged the night before, the aftertaste
>   of the dream I awoke from.

I had been called *Heir to Your Body* and passed on
to another pair of lips.

How mercantile, the communion.

How like a wafer, the coin,
my flesh.

NEVERBODY

Unsaid,
            but that the hand makes it
known, a gesture not yet clear, but veering
close, close.

And what else should speak for you then?

The sparrow
                caught in the soot-limed chimney,
its wings thrashing and thrashing and
thrashing —

What revealed then, what rent?

Bone, ivory, dentin —
                    the body's bright Braille to sift through
as harbinger, herald, or messenger — each a sign
almost certain

to assemble an architecture worthy of worship,

but that your livid offering,
                    the sparrow again enlivened, its parts
quickening to pronounce a way back, should
want only to linger or bide

or persist, uninterrupted, in this,
our marrow-house.

DEAR

1

Stand. As in trees. As in, I am standing near you
but cannot be seen.

          O screen of oak leaves, when will you turn
upon your red hinge? Soon there will be nothing left

but skeleton keys, winter, your finger trailing in dust.
It accumulates.

         Standing up, the knees give out first, filled
with their fluid. Then your voice, ravaged from such a distance.

We glimpse one another. We cannot speak.

We endure the melliferous drone of our folded hearts.

2

A swarm. Your heart the hive busy at work.
One body yields

        to the next, as they pass from chamber to chamber.
Somewhere in the vena cava a community stirs. They are hard at work.

The air turns viscous with their yellow light,
the light of their labor.

        As it dawns on them, the queen pulses with heat.
But she is still so far off. An entire life spent before reaching the spot.

How light travels, on the end of a dead signal.

DEAR ORPHEUS

Bright *allez oup*, the nightingale's munificent cry
would later be remembered as song,

                                but for now settles in the back of the throat
like a cough. Is not any haunt or prophecy this burden, as it passes

from one station to the next?

It provokes the mind to a culpability
hitherto unaware of——

                    these sheaves of music, this predilection to name.
When we arrived we were invited to invent one another in various forms.

Me, the lyre. You, the head absent its body.

FEATHERS OR A CROW ON A DEAD BIRD

Consider the immutable, what must have been,
before now, before this—

              The road a dark line. Your finger, our guide,
what interrupts. The blood still deepening (somehow) the pavement.

Registered or at least glimpsed, the form or shape or remains
have separated.

              It is not death, nor even (no) the bird, but (again, somehow)
its reproach—the mouth's open posture of disbelief, flight now

fluttering in my throat.

SCRAPE THAT STARTS THE FIRE

1

You keep others away to keep the wound
for yourself.

In your ardor,
                    it resembles a signal fire, a commotion
of spark and flame, an alarum meant to warn (again)

others away.

There is nothing now but the wound and its warmth

2

and you within it.

The way you are held
                    within it, a thing rubbed beyond
ardor, blush, rubescence, a figure meant to lose itself

along the way.

Your body, the shadow of the wound, the red
that runs

3

through everything.

HE CALLS ME LAMBENT, LUCENT

What I said, I said for fear of the fire.
— Joan of Arc

1

The days are embers lit in my throat. When I speak, the timid fire
that is my voice, erupts.

          When I am hushed, the dark coal collapses back
          into itself and nothing comes out.

The fire lasted for as long as I allowed it to sing.

Then it became a scattering of intermittent light that shone,
intermittently, upon my breast,

             a tableau vivant where my heart used to be.
I did not foresee my words becoming such a reverie of mimic and refrain.

Once I spoke, I dared not fetch them
from the flame.

2

We speak like matches in a mirror. Each flagrant reflection a portrait
of restraint.

There is so little to go on, each wooden stem only lasting so long.
Soon, we are ash and soot to be swept up and carried away.

An absence, a stain.

An occasion for memory.

There is no more resemblance to light, only the words
that continue to come out like bits of ash,

like a bird passing through
an uninhabitable flame.

3

Inseparable from the fire, your words take precedence over it.
What you have to tell me

                        begins as a half-lit flower,
                but then unfolds, erupts.

And although the air smokes with its petals, its holy perfume,
I can still make out your offer.

Overhead, I hear the shuttling of wings in the dark.

Your voice, a spark that goes on firing.

The fire not far off.

4

Head full of soot, I cannot give pardon to the wind that whips
my thoughts about.

Absorbed as I am, it isn't easy being led. I follow your chemical trace
through the sulfur pits.

> I will use their chimney smoke as vaporous crumbs
> to find my way back.

But if I return, I will burn everything that reminds me of you.

I will pretend the journey never took place, never left
its indelible blush in my skin.

Its fitful fever of *again*, *again*.

5

To pass with impunity through the flame.

The hand does not think so. Singed or else caught in a labyrinth
of orange and white,

        white and orange, its fingers
      cannot take hold.

Between cinder and flare we meet,
the alleged arsonists.

Is this warehouse on fire your love letter? Do the sirens add ornamentation
to your already engulfed voice?

          The conflagration of wings that are the others
     fleeing, do you mean to make them so brightly lit?

To give them your timid fuse, its promise
of touch?

PERFORATE

Swallows fly through a fresco.

What hems in around them is the air.

And the days seem happier
                        because they pass, pieced together
to resemble a habitable pattern.

Part real, part conjecture, we are about to become this
ability to touch.

There is no other resolve but to fill in.

*Down from the sky / Came Eros taking off his clothes / His shirt
of Phoenician red*

The closest possible rendering.

To have drawn such luck from the beggar's bowl.

THE FEVER CHART

Things to note, score: the body's uneven
temperature

       (rising and falling), the number of days
I have gone without meat, the visitors,

each perplexed, ashen face —

I told them,
       May God grant that I become nothing.
Then the fever (rising and falling) offered its black fruit,

and I ate.

       ~

The bedsores, or what I often mistake
for stigmata,

       the body incorporates, brings upon itself
such consequence, damage, that at this stand-still,

the fever heightening, that ache all inside now,
cannot, will not, break.

       ~

The vase, there, its flowers,

                     dying a little more each day.
I watch and keep count. How long? *Forty days, forty nights.*

And now more. More.

           ~

What is least accountable, this new
(but not for long) body,

               burgeoning, breaking, becoming
more each day its own death shroud and veil.

Behind, behind, the voice goes,
and I cannot follow.

          ~

Where it reaches

           and what it finds, both spare
and intimate, your voice, lifted from field and ditch, hearth
and table.

It is hard to seize what is.

Then I saw a landscape without me in it.

I cannot say with certainty
that I saw nothing.

APPETITE OF THE BEREAVED

Pain's slow drip.
The fox gnawing at its ankle, its Venetian red—

    how even this becomes derivative of nature.

Red, mercurial,
each effort replaced by more meat on the bone

to be devoured,
the even coat spoilt from the butchering—

    how quickly one red spot wells up into another.

The eventual
ease of self-mutilation, the tendon loosening.

And the snare bearing down with its metal grip—

    how often I have imagined the clatter.

But not enough,
not ever.

NEVERBODY

Called *torn*, *break-away*, *asunderer*.

SURFEIT INCENDIARY

Among the roseate, I saw a white hand descend into the glade

and pluck out a bloom. It was too soon,
its petals too tightly wound,

                            the white glove discarded, fingers flushed
from coaxing. It's always like this, voracious and dumb,

mutely signaling assistance. I saw you burning,
then only the burn.

                    I returned the flint and steel lent to me, expecting
another favor. I was told to look at the flowers in the yard,

to call them by your name. I burnt that also.

46

DEAD LETTER: THE VENERABLE BEDE

A gash runs sideways through
the letter. It widens as words do.

Circle of speech,

                     elucidation, its radius,
from the stone to its brokenness, smoke

and dispersion, the hand to the palm
to the lines within it,

                     comes dispatch:

The barbarians drive us to the sea,
and the sea drives us back

to the barbarians. Between these,
two deadly alternatives await,
drowning or slaughter.

The sleeveless errand—

man running from fire; man
running from waves; man
running from man—the remnant.

Their days spent thus, commiserating.

SEVER, STAUNCH

Asleep, the animal still
                    chases after its own
hunger—mouth a-shudder, the limbs

that leap, eyes searching along
the dark-veined walls

of its sleep.

Like a tapestry,
                interwoven and deep,
deep, there the prey hastens

still further into
its escape.

Random,
            the delivery of grace—
who chanced upon the snare, what body

made it its home.

Hinge and buckle,
                salvation's delay—you
are only here because I hurry toward you,

wanting to believe.

No choice but to follow
your bloodtrail,

deathbloom,
to find it sweet.

Wound in my mouth, I sidle past you,
through you

(how else should I live)

as I eat.

LIMINAL *(your voice so terribly human, its distance)*

Charged, the despotic fire banks.

(It was told to.)

Ash arches even further, its single shadow
listless, pre-determined.

Summoned by the great cloud, its remains scattered
in every direction, I stand neither here nor there.

The interminable space, the unbeliever.

Tell me to breathe.

THE WORD IN WHICH THE WOUND

Signet, marker,
                the mercurial upshot, blood spreading
and seized, the air my voice takes hold of, tongue

(now, always) wrestling forth—
                      do not thou strive in words—
but still in words it is achieved: communion, wedlock, the last invite
by which to please.

Summoned to conjoin,
                to give it speech, the word of him
leans, furtive, away—*the word of him not bound*—

but (now, again) uttered,
                thrown out, so that whatever remains,
this apprehension, the mouth's inevitable complaint (o forgive me),
is said, raised.

TO GATHER THE GRAPES OR DRY STICKS

1

Ruminate, remember.

To become acquainted with what is or what is not
or what could be or could not be the matter.

Enjoined, the two of us, coupled
as both reminder,

                    remembrancer.

Your body, now, bright white, visaged
and all the more stranger.

Your name, scavenged among us, now
(repeatedly) talked about,

sought after.

2

What I call you,

                  Comforter, Consoler. Dove
that alights upon that which cannot shake it loose —

the adored giving itself, unabashedly, over
to the adorer.

What I have only just begun to gather up
in my arms.

The stone rolled back.

Your body no longer.

3

All morning, this truancy.

And all along the way,
                         the tenantless road, offering
its promise of departure and return.

But what of arrival, its fortune, and those
who said their prayers to be counted

among the missing?

I am here and still no one has left.

4

What came before you
                           but the desire to reach
some terminus, the post or stone set

by which we recognize an end?

Now your hand is raised as in parting
or welcome.

Either way, it resembles,
                          from here, a bride's
half-turned face, which is turned (as it must)

to resemble (as it does) my own.

HYMENEAL

Scabfold, what beneath remains hidden,
unsolicited, myself.

        The bruised fruit deepening further into
    its already amaranthine calm, its joined

red with red, your touch——a hand reaching up
to the over-laden limb, the ache

now so belatedly
felt.

O TASTE AND SEE

The wound
inflicted,

      the rapture —

Pursued, pursued,
              like a dog continually returning
to the prey from which it has been driven.

Not deterred,
         nor disheartened even, the animal
impulse still worries the human surface,

or is, unbeknownst,
already obeyed.

            ~

So when the spear entered your side,
I waited.

What kind of withness is this?

When living in the body,
           being body, I take up
your dark and twin redness, endure
in its always torn and fed upon

shape—
        thou *dismembered*,
dismemberer.

        ~

Necessary, or else
           said to be so, the damage
made all the more real by my thirst for it.

Mouthful after mouthful,
the speechless act.

But let you taste and see.

WOUND SEQUENCE

Armature

Series of coils group of

wire a way of warning without words

through which our conversation is induced

come here and talk to me you who made my mind your home

coinage raised velum and tongue

the consonants formed and pausing a finger

pressed against my lips first there's and then

we must keep up our various ends

without each other we tear at each other

passing it back and forth.

Judas Kiss

Hands over   the rose of Sharon   as payment   voucher

the turgid yellow flower   that began as bud

became a tumor   burgeoning on its stem

a pallid thing   aberrant among the crowd   drawing near

pointing at your skin   how it does what it does

the life of it   ruddy wound opening closing

the sky rent   its saints disbanded

loosed from their casement

one by one

your body   its partition of bone.

Red Hymn

What breaks   so fervently loose

from the *traje de luces*   sequined with saints

their lights gone out   one after another

bearing nothing particular   but song   in particular

because everything said   is true

at least once   the *Veronica*   led the bull's head

away from you

though now   we watch

incredulous   the posture you hold

announcing   the horn   in your side.

In the Honeyed Head

Plagued mouth   spill your infestation   we grow

weary of waiting for the animal

to lay down   its remains

to slacken   make ready their bed

the hecatomb   the interred   the walk throughout them

brandishing honey in my cupped hands

out of the eater came forth   this meat   this man

out of the strong   a honeyed drone

and easing open the animal   its body eased upon

a knot   undone   to keep the dying away.

Caret

Omission   gradually   or by cessation

the herd passing in the midst of its breath   the stone dropped

through the surface   falling

what continues between   continues

when the wheel turns   so much loadstone   cinder and chaff

handfuls of ballast come loose   and rolling to a stop

how far we have come

not to rectify but to render   collusion

a body up and going about its   advent.

SOJOURNER

Taut and unyielding (but a little, a little) the gristle-
creak, wings swelled,

                    an arch of muscle and bone spread
(but a little) wider and still (a little) wider, until

what beneath, what lying in
your shadow is—

an occasion for *soul* or *spirit* or *stay*.

LET THIS CUP PASS FROM ME

That the body blames itself
for its own unrest.

        That desire has nowhere else to go
but into blood and skin and bone, into *must* and

have.

        ~

That the leaves of the fig tree appear
only after its fruit,

        that Christ made it that way as punishment
for his hunger, unabated, when he reached Jerusalem

the fig tree had nothing to offer.

The body wants and does not wait
            for an answer, but continues on
into each new desire, until, withered at both ends, from ravishment,
from disappointment, from more or less desire,

I meet, in the middle, you.

        ~

That you come, green and unbidden,
before your heralding,

        the leaves you pass through, retreat back into,
not there, not yet, but only appear after you have left, as if to promise a return,

as if, more likely, awaiting
another gift.

LONG DARNING NEEDLES' HINT OF SUTURE

How we want
          and then become, so easily and without blame, without knowing even,
what we want: juncture between two bodies, whorls of a gastropod shell,

joint or line articulated, we remain seam-like, threading our way
toward stitch.

USURY (*the heart, its gift and acquisition*)

Love, interrupting solitude, grants
forgiveness,

       where before the body sought to conceal
whatever wound lay despondent in its side. A flower

perhaps, of another sort, though its bloom
through the bandage

       resembles, almost immediately, that of the rose
on its stem. It is this we speak of (the rose), more often than others,

and have come to understand, long before
the interruption

       of love. The salient color now conjured
up in the mind, the mind working it into a further brilliance,

the likeness it holds. How it comes to bear it
(the wound), without effort,

       every time. How it becomes, inevitably,
an image for the mind to use when in the absence of love.

Or, closer still, within its confines, the wish to wear
our blood like (the red) roses do.

CHURCH OF THE VOLATILE ALKALI

Promiscuous, air is air. Nothing falls through
its sundry.

      For days we starved in small clusters, compared only
to the saguaro's blossom, its adoration diminished along all fifteen feet

of its one green stem.

Once our instruments reached their dead end,
distance was dead reckoned.

        We came to the column of swirling dust
and spoke to the clamor. We made an altar of breath

breathing there.

MAKESHIFT (*your kingdom, its currency*)

Because I wish to prostrate myself, you will spend me
to make more money.
                        You will live forever within the fiduciary act,
isolate, a sentry, the one
who counts on his fingers the dull and glinting money.

Because you starve
                        without my money, the hunger begins
in your palm, its ruddy purse
opening and closing (always) on money. You will pull
the drawstrings tight,
                        you will continue to clutch it to your breast,
the spent and unspent money.

Because I borrow of myself to pay for myself, because
I make good money,
                        you will choose me over the rest. You will
fill the ledger, my heart,
abundant (always) with your script.

APOLOGIA

Errant

Your hand   having affixed awhile my life   opens

in one direction only   came the bovine rose

from its bough

a thing for singing to   for slaughter   invocation

of the beloved   the sacrifice   of one so partial

this part rather than the whole   body

received as gift or money   what others might have called

alms   this my flower   offering

its involute petals   every which way   lulled to the parting.

O Miracle of Our Empty Hands

The question   used to separate   a part of

your hands   full of holding

came back with so much   the flower

placed in your hair   another name to remember

stamen   stigma   style

the trestle aslant

and someone climbing down   rung after rung

excuses became   parenthetical

one does not possess   we are told   one gives

wherefore you shall know me   another name.

Cut Flower Garden

Ecumenical   the tumult   its crowd of petals

tourmaline   and of a great beauty when cut

they desire nothing   coveting one another

we came to appreciate each other   forever

for a while   for as long as it lasts

stalks bleed wet sugar

filling   fit to burst   a globule

beaded along the blade

what we return   remainder   scrap and trim

shrugged off   the loosed casing.

Fought

Slack and dryspell of thirst

it's hard to tell   what they're saying

squeezed tight like that   the unapproachable roses

finally   eased themselves open

and spoke more plainly

I heard the latch make its latch noise

the wide and widening of the forgotten

and expected someone   behind me

an unfamiliar voice asking to shake on it

together   our hands   a lantern swinging.

Mantilla

Labial of wind   pursed but no longer a sound

this engine of breath   small words in print

alighting   someone came down

if only to shrive   the mist

and waking from the dream   make room for the dream

water   vapor   or mist

image not the image   however circuitous

the bangle of condensation   it held

words   stray light

the motion of this   going on like this.

NUMEN

Provocation, voicelet,
                   what moves in me awaits
credulity, a torn sheet in which to wrap its weight.

Solicitous attendant, o pilgrim, from the charnel
house you must transpire,

a shudder, a complaint.

        ~

What stirs is not ancestry.

Nor the inception of any one blood.

But the insistence to wake,
                   to bear witness, comes
as a stranger, from no one's mouth, no
other arrangement.

        ~

Your tongue, speech-pocked, unnerved, a whip
circling overhead.

My body forced to it, listening and
listening.

The imagined crack, its hiss, or what
it might have said:

> *let those believe who may.*

A summons
> *(let those believe)* that gathers
to itself a certainty, *(let those believe
who may)* the more

it leaves one behind.

> ~

And belief now an unrest, growing
singly in search of a pair,

the absence of some other, your voice calling
out to me —

> *skeptic, refuser, Thomas' head*
> *as it continues to shake.*

(know this)

I would not be here without you.

THE LARK, ITS SPUR

Image of flight,
                the horizon there but for the eye
to follow, a dark spot flitting hither and hither.

My hands, hooked at the thumbs, each
finger meant to lift,

                to leave, to liken the body
to what it cannot possibly possess.

And waits.

And does.

COME HITHER

Without regret, leave.

Or wait for water to collect
and overwhelm any evidence or your ever having been

here.

There is no other way. We lift ourselves
beyond the casualties

of what came before (the flood, the swollen river, its overrunning),
and kneel, enclosed, in a departure of sorts,

                              now that each body has been placed
                    into its ark and sped away.

                    ~

I hear you
still,

so close the silence full of water, what rocks
beneath us, what is shared between,

                    heavy breaths that pull at the air as against ropes,
            each cinch tightened and relaxed, tightened and—

                    ~

The weather vane courses on through the sludge,
its wings flapping with the current.

What man couldn't fix, you, Lord, had,
and now the sediment

            loosed as carelessly as a sack of seed split,
      spilled—there is no recovery from such loss.

      ~

Dark-fumed,
          the water now receding, now pulling us back.
Visit or visitation, whatever was meant
to warn through drowning.

We expect honeycomb and locusts, sign and wonder,
but this corruptible

          moldhouse, this fleshrot, wormwhorl, the finger of you, Lord,
beckons, draws forward, lays upon the body its burden,

makes it
heavy with water.

      ~

Baptism never seemed so deep, the head
pushed still further under,

                    each embrace substantiating faith or surrender,
        the senseless body floating among the waves' incantation.

                ~

Who will draw you out, now
that you've given yourself over?

                        Who dissolve
your body like a host on their tongue?

What stopping place will be provided, what
rest?

Where am I in this emergence—
who comes?

The italicized lines in "Called Back, Called Back" are from 1 Samuel 3:1-18.

Some of the italicized lines in "My Easter" are taken from Mark 14:27-51.

"Straight *(not straight, and broken lines)*" comes from the title of a painting by Sol LeWitt.

The italicized lines in "The Wound in Which the Word" come from John 20:27.

The italicized lines in the first "Hymeneal" are from Othello, Act 5, scene ii: "When I have plucked thy rose / I cannot give it vital growth again, / It needs must wither. I'll smell thee on the tree."

The title "He Calls Me Lambent, Lucent" comes from a line in Rachel Zucker's *Eating in the Underworld*.

"He Calls Me Lambent, Lucent" corrupts and attenuates the following lines by Paul Valery: "Nothing so pure can coexist with the circumstances of life / We only traverse the idea of perfection as a hand passes / With impunity through a flame; but the flame is uninhabitable."

In "Perforate," the italicized lines are from Guy Davenport's translation of Sappho.

"The Fever Chart" contains quotes from Simone Weil's *Gravity and Grace*.

In "Dead Letter: The Venerable Bede," the italicized lines are taken from Bede's *The Ecclesiastical History of the English People*.

The italicized lines in "The Word in Which the Wound" are from Timothy 2:2.

"Wound Sequence" contains the phrase *traje de luces*, which translates from the Spanish as "suit of lights" and refers to the costume worn by bullfighters. The Veronica is a bullfighting pass whereby the cape is drawn over the bull's head while the matador remains in place. The reference in the poem is to Saint Veronica, who offered a napkin to Christ while he proceeded to his crucifixion.

ACKNOWLEDGMENTS

Thanks to the editors of the following journals in which some of these poems or versions of these poems first appeared: *can we have our ball back*, *The Colorado Review*, *Denver Quarterly*, *Diagram*, *Fine Madness*, *GutCult*, *The Iowa Review*, *Interim*, *The Journal*, *The Laurel Review*, *lyric poetry review*, *Memorious*, *New Orleans Review*, *Phoebe*, *Pleiades*, *River City*, *Southeast Review*, and *Verse*.

Many thanks also to my readers and mentors: Chad Parmenter, Kent Shaw, Chief, Jesse Watt, Steve Schreiner, Donald Finkel, David Hamilton, Claudia Keelan, Brenda Hillman, John Gallaher, and Matthew Cooperman.

Deepest gratitude to Ulrike Termeer for her enthusiasm and generosity, and to the Nightboat editors for their early and enduring support. And to Glenn Schaeffer for his patronage.

ABOUT THE AUTHOR

Joshua Kryah was born and raised in St. Louis, Missouri. A graduate of the Iowa Writers' Workshop, he received a Ph.D. from the University of Nevada, Las Vegas, where he was a Schaeffer Fellow in poetry. He lives in Las Vegas with his wife and daughter. More work can be found at www.joshuakryah.com.

ABOUT THE ARTIST

For more than twenty years, Marcel Proust's *Remembrance of Things Past* has been the inspiration for Ulrike Termeer's art. Born in 1949 in Germany, Termeer attempts to capture on canvas what Proust sought to capture in words—an elusive reality of involuntary memory, where coincidence and unforeseeable remembrance collide and converge. This intersection of time and unconscious is revealed in Termeer's layers of interlocking line, color, and undecipherable script, often appearing on diverse tactile media or hand-made paper. Termeer created the cover and interior art especially for *Glean*, deconstructing Caravaggio's classic work "Doubting Thomas" to mirror the way Kryah's words explore the subject in his poem "Numen". Her work is in permanent collections at several of Germany's top museums. For more about the artist visit www.ulriketermeer.de.

ABOUT NIGHTBOAT BOOKS

Nightboat Books, a nonprofit organization, seeks to develop audiences for writers whose work resists convention and transcends boundaries. We publish books rich with poignancy, intelligence, and risk.

Please visit our web site, www.nightboat.org, to learn more about us and how you can support our mission and future publications.

The following individuals have supported the publication of this book. We thank them for their generosity and commitment to the mission of Nightboat Books:

Heidi Arnold
Jennifer Chapis
Katherine Dimma
Sarah Heller
Daniel Lin
James Muldoon
Rebecca Newth
James and Carolyn Patterson
Beverly Rogers
Anonymous (4)

Nightboat Books also thanks Kory Riesterer for her contributions to the production of this book.

SEPTEMBER 2007

The Sorrow and the Fast of It, Nathalie Stephens

The Sorrow and the Fast of It exists in a middle place: an overlay of indistinct geographies and trajectories. Strained between the bodies of Nathalie and Nathanaël, between dissolution and abjection, between the borders that limit the body in its built environment—the city and its name(s), the countries, the border crossings—the narrative, splintered and fractured, dislocates its own compulsion. This text addresses the maddened and the maddening, but what is madness away from the language(s) that might enclose it? *The Sorrow and the Fast of It* is the first U.S. publication from Nathalie Stephens (Nathanaël), a Canadian writer of over ten intergenre, experimental works, including *Touch to Affliction*, *Paper City*, and *Je Nathanaël*.

DECEMBER 2007

Selected Poems, Michael Burkard

The volume collects early poems by a poet both spiritually haunted and grimly determined to live in the world. Burkard, the author of ten books of poetry, adds a section of previously uncollected work to poems from *In a White Light*, *Ruby for Grief*, *The Fires They Kept*, *Fictions from the Self*, and *None, River*.